Easy Tomatillos Cookbook

A Tomatillo Cookbook Filled with 50 Delicious Tomatillo Recipes

By
BookSumo Press
All rights reserved

Published by
http://www.booksumo.com

ENJOY THE RECIPES?

KEEP ON COOKING WITH 6 MORE FREE COOKBOOKS!

Visit our website and simply enter your email address to join the club and receive your 6 cookbooks.

http://booksumo.com/magnet

https://www.instagram.com/booksumopress/

https://www.facebook.com/booksumo/

LEGAL NOTES

All Rights Reserved. No Part Of This Book May Be Reproduced Or Transmitted In Any Form Or By Any Means. Photocopying, Posting Online, And / Or Digital Copying Is Strictly Prohibited Unless Written Permission Is Granted By The Book's Publishing Company. Limited Use Of The Book's Text Is Permitted For Use In Reviews Written For The Public.

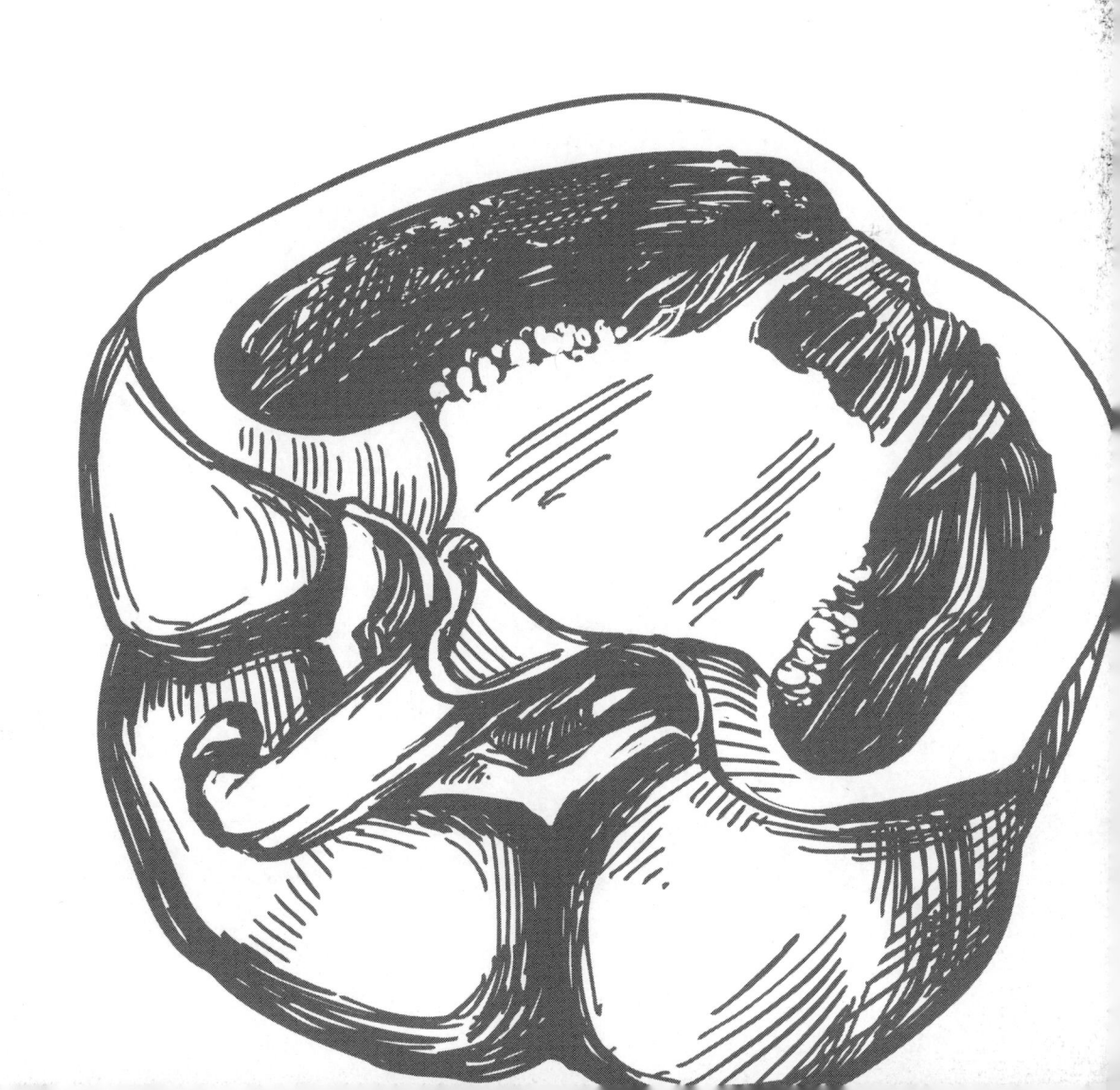

Table of Contents

Azteca Soup 7

Authentic Mexican Salsa Verde 8

East LA Guacamole 9

Summer Evening Tomato and Fruit Pie 10

Zacatecas Chicken 11

Super-Hot Fire Salsa 12

Late Spring Tilapia 13

Ecuadorian Inspired Chutney 15

6-Ingredient Dip 17

Easy Fried Tomatoes 18

Central American Chicken Platter 19

Fruity Guacamole 20

5 Star Salsa 21

Muenster and Chili Chicken 22

Tuesday Barcelona Dinner 24

November's Tacos 25

Restaurant-Style Salsa 26

Working Woman's Favorite Chili 28

Guadalajara Steak 29

Traditional Mexican Pie 30

Authentic Latin Dinner Chicken 31

Southwestern Tomatillos 32

Sizzling Skillet Shrimp 33

Cancun Breakfast 34

Salsa Festival 35

Late June Salsa 36

Mexican Cilantro Appetizer 37

Chipotle Salmon 38

New Mexican Lunch Rice 39

Creamy Tomatillo Topping or Dip 40

Easy Chicken Stew 41

The Best Salsa Ever! 42

Tamale Cakes with Southwest Sauce 43

South American Tacos 45

San Miguel de Allende Shrimp 46

Southwestern Burgers 47

Vegetarian Mexican Casserole 49

Mexico City Green Enchiladas 51

Rural Mexican Breakfast Eggs 53

Sakura's Japanese Salsa 54

Tamale Bake 55

Orange Serrano Salmon on Grill 57

Mexican Mango Salsa 58

Deep Fried Avocado 59

Chicken Tortillas with Spicy Chocolate Sauce 60

Mexican Style Salad Dressing 62

Azteca Soup

Prep Time: 20 mins
Total Time: 1 hr 40 mins

Servings per Recipe: 6
Calories   159 kcal
Fat   10.1 g
Carbohydrates   7.4g
Protein   10.5 g
Cholesterol   27 mg
Sodium   43 mg

Ingredients

2 skinless, boneless chicken breast halves, flattened
3 tbsp olive oil
1 onion, chopped
3 cloves garlic, minced
1 lb. chopped tomatillos
2 jalapeno peppers, seeded and minced
4 C. chicken stock
1/4 tsp cayenne pepper
1/2 tsp hot pepper sauce
2 tbsp chopped fresh cilantro
1/4 C. sour cream (optional)
salt to taste
ground black pepper to taste

Directions

1. In a large pan, heat the oil on high heat and sear the chicken for about 2 minutes per side.
2. Transfer the chicken into a plate and keep aside.
3. In the same pan, add the onions and garlic and sauté till golden.
4. Stir in the tomatillos, jalapeño peppers and broth and bring to a boil.
5. Reduce the heat and simmer, covered for about 15 minutes.
6. In a food processor, add the tomatillo mixture in batches and pulse till smooth.
7. Return the pureed mixture to pan and cook till heated completely.
8. Add the cayenne pepper and hot pepper sauce.
9. Cut the chicken into thin slices and then shred it.
10. Add the shredded chicken, salt and pepper and remove from the heat.
11. Divide the soup into the serving bowls.
12. Stir in the cilantro in each bowl and serve with a dollop of the sour cream.

AUTHENTIC Mexican Salsa Verde

Prep Time: 10 mins
Total Time: 25 mins

Servings per Recipe: 8
Calories	24 kcal
Fat	0.6 g
Carbohydrates	4.6 g
Protein	0.8 g
Cholesterol	0 mg
Sodium	439 mg

Ingredients

- 1 lb. tomatillos, husked
- 1/2 C. finely chopped onion
- 1 tsp minced garlic
- 1 serrano chili peppers, minced
- 2 tbsp chopped cilantro
- 1 tbsp chopped fresh oregano
- 1/2 tsp ground cumin
- 1 1/2 tsp salt
- 2 C. water

Directions

1. In a pan, add the tomatillos, onion, garlic, chili pepper, cilantro, oregano, cumin, salt and water on high heat and bring to a boil.
2. Reduce the heat to medium-low and simmer for about 10-15 minutes.
3. In a blender, add the tomatillos mixture in batches and pulse till smooth.

East LA Guacamole

🥣 Prep Time: 20 mins
🕐 Total Time: 25 mins

Servings per Recipe: 24
Calories   48 kcal
Fat   3.8 g
Carbohydrates   3.7 g
Protein   0.7 g
Cholesterol   0 mg
Sodium   3 mg

Ingredients

6 fresh tomatillos, husks discarded and tomatillos rinsed
1 white onion, quartered
2 cloves garlic
2 jalapeno peppers, seeded if desired
water, to cover
salt to taste
1/4 C. chopped fresh cilantro
1 tbsp fresh lime juice
3 ripe avocados, halved lengthwise and pitted

Directions

1. In a pan, add the tomatillos, onion, garlic, jalapeño peppers and enough water to cover on medium heat and bring them to a boil.
2. Reduce the heat and simmer for about 5-8 minutes.
3. With a slotted spoon, transfer the tomatillos mixture into a blender in batches and pulse till smooth.
4. Add the salt, cilantro and lime juice and pulse for a few seconds to mix.
5. Scoop out the avocado flesh and transfer into the blender and pulse till well combined.

SUMMER EVENING
Tomato and Fruit Pie

Prep Time: 20 mins
Total Time: 1 hr 25 mins

Servings per Recipe: 8
Calories 470 kcal
Fat 20.2 g
Carbohydrates 70.9 g
Protein 4 g
Cholesterol 11 mg
Sodium 266 mg

Ingredients

1 pastry for 9-inch double crust pie
3 C. sliced ripe tomatillos
3 C. sliced strawberries
1/4 C. instant tapioca
1 1/2 C. white sugar
1 tsp lemon juice
3 tbsp butter, sliced

Directions

1. Set your oven to 400 degrees F before doing anything else.
2. Place 1 pie crust into a 9-inch pie dish and gently, press to set.
3. In a bowl, mix together the tomatillos, strawberries, tapioca, sugar and lemon juice.
4. Keep aside for about 15 minutes, stirring occasionally.
5. Place the tomatillo-strawberry mixture into the prepared pie crust and top with the butter slices.
6. Cover the pie with the second pie crust and pinch the edges to seal.
7. Cut the slits into the top crust for ventilation.
8. Arrange the pie onto a baking sheet.
9. Cook in the oven for about 50 minutes.

Zacatecas Chicken

Prep Time: 10 mins
Total Time: 30 mins

Servings per Recipe: 4
Calories	487 kcal
Fat	33.7 g
Carbohydrates	7.1 g
Protein	37.8 g
Cholesterol	108 mg
Sodium	198 mg

Ingredients

- 1 (3 1/2) lb. whole chicken, cut into 6 pieces
- 1 lb. fresh tomatillos, husks removed
- 2 dried California chili pods
- 3 dried red chili peppers
- 2 tbsp olive oil
- salt to taste

Directions

1. Set your oven to 350 degrees F before doing anything else.
2. In a small roasting pan, place the tomatillos, California chilies and red chili peppers.
3. Cook in the oven for about 20 minutes, turning occasionally.
4. Remove from the oven and transfer the tomatillo mixture and salt into a food processor and pulse till smooth.
5. In a large skillet, heat the oil on medium-high heat and sear the chicken pieces till golden brown.
6. Stir in the tomatillo mixture.
7. Reduce the heat to medium-low and simmer, covered for about 20-25 minutes.

SUPER-HOT
Fire Salsa

🥣 Prep Time: 10 mins
🕐 Total Time: 35 mins

Servings per Recipe: 12
Calories   18 kcal
Fat   0.4 g
Carbohydrates   3.5g
Protein   0.6 g
Cholesterol   0 mg
Sodium   50 mg

Ingredients

1 lb. tomatillos, unhusked
2 serrano chili peppers
2 jalapeno chili peppers
8 pequin chili peppers
4 cloves garlic
1 small whole onion, peeled
1/4 C. chopped cilantro
salt to taste

Directions

1. Heat a dry, cast iron pan on medium-high heat and cook the tomatillos, chilis, garlic cloves and onion till the husks of the tomatillos have blackened and their skins turn translucent, flipping occasionally.
2. Transfer the tomatillo mixture into a bowl and keep aside to cool slightly.
3. Remove the husks from the tomatillos and the stems from the chili peppers.
4. In a food processor, add the tomatillos, chili peppers, cilantro and salt and pulse till desired consistency.
5. Transfer the salsa into a pan on medium heat and cook for about 5 minutes.

Late Spring Tilapia

Prep Time: 25 mins
Total Time: 50 mins

Servings per Recipe: 4
Calories	213 kcal
Fat	7.2 g
Carbohydrates	12.4g
Protein	24.7 g
Cholesterol	41 mg
Sodium	68 mg

Ingredients

- cooking spray
- 1 large red bell pepper, seeds removed and pepper quartered lengthwise
- 2 tsp canola oil
- 1 C. husked, cored and chopped tomatillos
- salt and ground black pepper to taste
- 1 clove garlic, minced
- 1/4 C. chopped fresh parsley
- 2 tbsp rice vinegar
- 1 tsp honey
- 2 tbsp all-purpose flour
- 2 tsp chili powder
- 1 tsp dried oregano
- 4 tilapia fillets
- 2 tsp canola oil
- 1 lemon, halved and seeds removed
- 1 sprig fresh cilantro, chopped (optional)

Directions

1. Set the broiler of your oven and arrange oven rack about 6-inches from the heating element.
2. Line a baking sheet with a greased piece of the foil.
3. Arrange the pepper pieces, cut sides down onto the prepared baking sheet.
4. Cook under the broiler for about 5-10 minutes.
5. Transfer the blackened pepper pieces into a bowl.
6. Immediately with a plastic wrap, cover the bowl tightly and keep aside for about 20 minutes.
7. Remove the skins of the pepper pieces and discard.
8. In a large nonstick skillet, heat 2 tsp of the canola oil on medium heat and cook the tomatillos for about 8 minutes.
9. Stir in the salt, black pepper and garlic and cook for about 1 minute.
10. In a blender, add the hot tomatillos, roasted red pepper, parsley, rice vinegar and honey and pulse till smooth.

11. In a shallow bowl, mix together the flour, chili powder, and dried oregano.
12. Season the fish fillets with the salt and black pepper and coat with the flour mixture evenly.
13. In a skillet, heat 2 tsp of the canola oil on medium-high heat and cook the fish fillets for about 2-3 minutes.
14. Carefully flip the side and cook for about 4 minutes.
15. Transfer the fish fillets into a serving platter.
16. Serve with a drizzling of the lemon juice alongside the pan sauce.

Ecuadorian Inspired Chutney

Prep Time: 30 mins
Total Time: 1 hr 45 mins

Servings per Recipe: 25
Calories   135 kcal
Fat   0.6 g
Carbohydrates   32.8g
Protein   1.3 g
Cholesterol   0 mg
Sodium   61 mg

Ingredients

- 5 C. chopped green tomatoes
- 4 C. fresh tomatillos, husked, rinsed, and chopped
- 1 1/2 C. golden raisins
- 1 1/2 C. chopped onion
- 2 1/4 C. packed brown sugar
- 1/2 tsp salt
- 1 3/4 C. apple cider vinegar
- 1 1/2 tbsp pickling spice
- 1 1/2 tsp chili powder
- 2 tbsp finely chopped crystallized ginger
- 1 tbsp brown mustard seed
- 5 (1 pint) canning jars with lids and rings

Directions

1. In a large pan, add the green tomatoes, tomatillos, raisins, onion, brown sugar, salt, apple cider vinegar, pickling spice, chili powder, crystallized ginger and brown mustard seed on medium heat and bring to a boil.
2. Cook, stirring continuously till the brown sugar is dissolved.
3. Reduce heat and simmer for about 1-2 hours, stirring occasionally.
4. In a pan of boiling water, sterilize the jars and lids for at least 5 minutes.
5. Place the chutney into the hot, sterilized jars, filling the jars to within 1/4-inch of the top.
6. Run a knife around the insides of the jars to remove any air bubbles.
7. With a moist paper towel, wipe the rims of the jars to remove any food residue.
8. Top with the lids and screw on rings.
9. In the bottom of a large pan, arrange a rack and fill halfway with the water.
10. Bring to a boil on high heat.
11. Carefully with a holder, place the jars into the pan, leaving a 2-inch space between the jars.
12. Add more boiling water if necessary till the water level is at least 1-inch above the tops of the jars.

13. Again, bring to a full boil and process, covered for about 15-20 minutes.
14. Remove the jars from the pan and place onto a wood surface, several inches apart to cool completely.
15. After cooling with a finger, press the top of each lid.
16. Store in a cool, dark area.

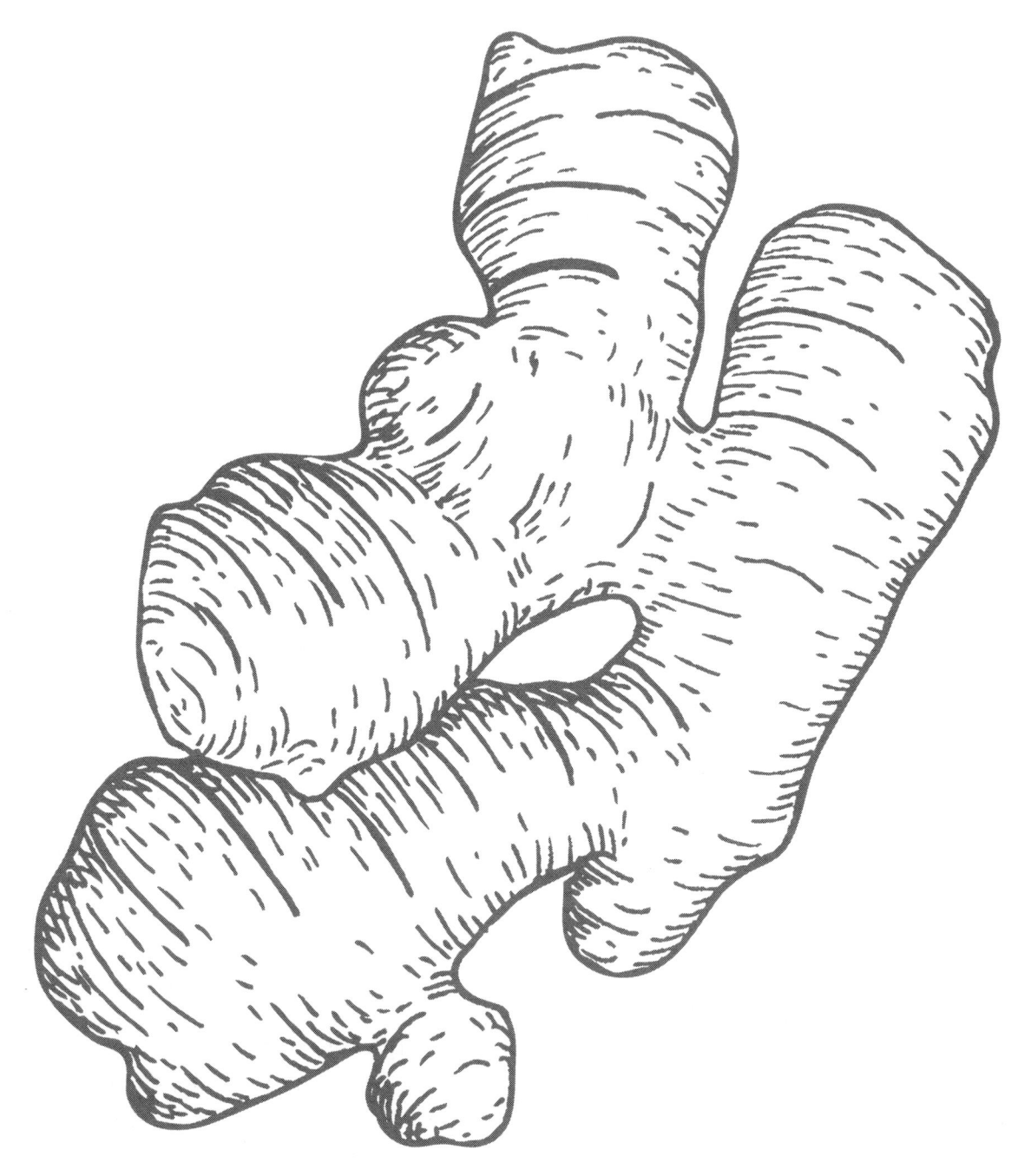

6-Ingredient Dip

Prep Time: 10 mins
Total Time: 15 mins

Servings per Recipe: 8
Calories	92 kcal
Fat	7.7 g
Carbohydrates	6.4g
Protein	1.4 g
Cholesterol	0 mg
Sodium	151 mg

Ingredients

- 7 oz. fresh tomatillos, husks discarded and tomatillos rinsed
- 1/4 C. thickly sliced white onion
- 1 fresh jalapeno chili
- 1/2 C. packed fresh cilantro sprigs
- 2 Hass avocados
- 1/2 tsp salt

Directions

1. In a small pan, add the tomatillos, onion and jalapeño and enough water to cover and bring to a boil.
2. Cook for about 5 minutes.
3. Drain and run under cold water to stop the cooking, then again drain well.
4. Half the jalapeño lengthwise and scrape out ribs and seeds, then cut into thick slices.
5. In a food processor, add the tomatillo mixture and cilantro and pulse till chopped finely but small chunks remain.
6. Half the avocados lengthwise and discard the pits.
7. Scoop out the flesh and transfer into a bowl.
8. With a fork, mash the avocado and salt till chunky.
9. Fold in the tomatillo mixture and serve.

EASY
Fried Tomatoes

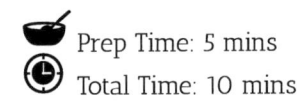

🥣 Prep Time: 5 mins
🕙 Total Time: 10 mins

Servings per Recipe: 4
Calories   133 kcal
Fat   7.7 g
Carbohydrates   13.4g
Protein   3.4 g
Cholesterol   0 mg
Sodium   256 mg

Ingredients

2 egg white, lightly beaten
1/3 C. cornmeal
1/2 tsp herbs de Provence
1/2 tsp garlic salt
ground black pepper to taste

8 tomatillos, husked and sliced 1/4 inch thick
2 tbsp vegetable oil

Directions

1. In a shallow bowl, add the egg whites.
2. In another shallow bowl, mix together the cornmeal, herbs, salt and pepper.
3. Dip the tomatillo slices in egg whites and then coat with the cornmeal mixture evenly.
4. In a skillet, heat the oil on medium heat and fry the tomatillo slices for about 2-3 minutes per side.
5. Serve immediately.

Central American Chicken Platter

Prep Time: 15 mins
Total Time: 1 hr 15 mins

Servings per Recipe: 4
Calories	334 kcal
Fat	13.2 g
Carbohydrates	23.6 g
Protein	31.5 g
Cholesterol	68 mg
Sodium	384 mg

Ingredients

- 3 fresh Poblano chili peppers
- 3 Anaheim chili peppers
- 3/4 lb. tomatillos, diced
- 1 onion, chopped
- 2/3 C. red bell pepper, diced
- 4 green onions, chopped
- 6 cloves garlic, minced
- 1 C. chicken broth
- 3 tbsp vegetable oil
- 4 skinless, boneless chicken breast halves - cut into 2 inch pieces
- 1/4 C. all-purpose flour
- 1 tbsp dried oregano
- 1/2 tsp salt
- 1 pinch black pepper
- 1 pinch cayenne pepper
- 2/3 C. fresh cilantro, chopped

Directions

1. Set your oven to 450 degrees F before doing anything else.
2. Roast the peppers for about 25 minutes.
3. Remove the skin of peppers and then chop them.
4. In a pan, add the chopped peppers with tomatillos, onion, red pepper, green onion, garlic and chicken broth and bring to a boil.
5. Reduce the heat and simmer for 15 minutes.
6. Coat the chicken with the flour evenly.
7. In a large skillet, heat the oil on medium heat and sauté the chicken briefly.
8. Place the tomatillo mixture over the chicken.
9. Stir in the oregano, salt, black pepper and cayenne pepper and simmer for about 25 minutes.
10. Stir in the cilantro just before serving.

FRUITY
Guacamole

Prep Time: 15 mins
Total Time: 1 hr 15 mins

Servings per Recipe: 8
Calories   98 kcal
Fat   7.5 g
Carbohydrates   8.7g
Protein   1.3 g
Cholesterol   0 mg
Sodium   55 mg

Ingredients

2 ripe Hass avocados - halved, pitted, and peeled
2 tomatillos, husked and chopped
1 ripe mango - peeled, seeded, and cut into cubes
1/2 small red onion, finely chopped
1 Serrano chili pepper, finely chopped
2 tbsp chopped fresh cilantro
1 tbsp chopped fresh mint
1 1/2 tbsp fresh lemon juice
kosher salt to taste

Directions

1. In a bowl, add the avocado and salt and with a fork, mash till slightly chunky.
2. Add the tomatillos, mango, onion, Serrano chili pepper, cilantro, mint, lemon juice and salt and gently mix.
3. Place a plastic wrap over the surface of the guacamole and refrigerate for at least 1 hour.

5 Star Salsa

Prep Time: 15 mins
Total Time: 15 mins

Servings per Recipe: 6
Calories	87 kcal
Fat	7.3 g
Carbohydrates	6.4 g
Protein	1.3 g
Cholesterol	0 mg
Sodium	5 mg

Ingredients

- 6 oz. fresh tomatillos - husked, rinsed, and halved
- 1 tbsp thinly sliced serrano chilis
- 1 large ripe avocado - halved, seeded, and flesh scooped out of peel
- 1/4 C. packed cilantro leaves
- 1/2 lime, juiced
- salt to taste

Directions

1. In a food processor, add the tomatillos, Serrano pepper, avocado, cilantro, lime juice and salt and pulse till smooth.
2. Transfer the salsa into a serving bowl and serve.

MUENSTER
and Chili Chicken

🥣 Prep Time: 20 mins
🕐 Total Time: 6 hrs 50 mins

Servings per Recipe: 8
Calories   399 kcal
Fat   19.1 g
Carbohydrates   21.8g
Protein   33.4 g
Cholesterol   98 mg
Sodium   948 mg

Ingredients

1.5 C. chicken broth
1/2 C. teriyaki sauce
1 tbsp chili powder
1 tsp garlic powder
8 skinless, boneless chicken breast halves
8 slices Muenster cheese
3 1/2 lb. fresh tomatillos, husks removed
1/2 C. water
1 onion, chopped
6 cloves garlic, chopped
1 pinch salt and ground black pepper to taste
1/4 C. chopped fresh cilantro
1 C. sour cream

Directions

1. In a bowl, add the broth, teriyaki sauce, chili powder and garlic powder and beat till well combined.
2. Transfer the broth mixture into a resealable plastic bag.
3. Add the chicken and coat with the marinade generously.
4. Squeeze out the excess air and seal the bag tightly.
5. Refrigerator for about 6-24 hours.
6. Set your outdoor grill for medium-high heat and lightly, grease the grill grate.
7. Remove chicken from the bag and shake off the excess marinade.
8. Cook the chicken breasts on grill for about 7-10 minutes per side.
9. Arrange the chicken breasts in a baking dish and place a Muenster cheese slice over each breast.
10. Set your oven to 350 degrees F.
11. In a large pan, add the tomatillos and water and bring to a boil.
12. Reduce the heat to medium-low and simmer, covered for about 7-10 minutes.

13. Stir in the onion and garlic, salt and pepper and simmer for about 15 minutes.
14. In a blender, add the tomatillo sauce mixture and pulse till smooth.
15. Stir in the sour cream and cilantro into the tomatillo mixture.
16. Place the tomatillo mixture over the chicken and Muenster cheese evenly.
17. Cook in the oven for about 15 minutes.

TUESDAY
Barcelona Dinner

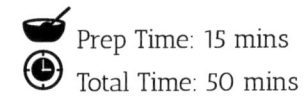

Prep Time: 15 mins
Total Time: 50 mins

Servings per Recipe: 8
Calories   528 kcal
Fat   35.1 g
Carbohydrates   27.2g
Protein   26.5 g
Cholesterol   68 mg
Sodium   1078 mg

Ingredients

1/2 lb. dry lentils
1 cube chicken bouillon
1/2 (1 lb.) Mexican chorizo, casing removed and meat crumbled
6 slices turkey bacon
1 Roma (plum) tomato, diced
1 tomatillo, diced
1 small white onion, diced
2 cloves garlic, minced
1/2 C. water
1/2 bunch cilantro, chopped
1/8 tsp cumin
5 tsp crumbled cotija cheese, divided
5 tsp sour cream, divided

Directions

1. Rinse the lentils and transfer into a large pan.
2. Add the chicken bouillon cube and enough water to cover the lentils by 2-inch and bring to a boil.
3. Simmer for about 20 minutes.
4. Meanwhile in a large skillet, heat on medium-high heat and cook the chorizo for about 10-15 minutes. Transfer the chorizo into a plate.
5. In the same pan, cook the bacon for about 5 minutes.
6. Transfer the bacon into a plate, leaving the drippings in pan. Chop the bacon.
7. In the same pan, add the tomato, tomatillo, onion and garlic and cook for about 5 minutes.
8. Stir in the water and cilantro and transfer the mixture into a blender and pulses till smooth.
9. In the pan of the lentils, add the pureed vegetables, cooked chorizo, cooked bacon and cumin on medium heat and cook for about 5 minutes.
10. Divide the lentils mixture in bowls and serve with a topping of the cotija cheese and a dollop of sour cream.

November's Tacos

Prep Time: 20 mins
Total Time: 45 mins

Servings per Recipe: 8
Calories	602 kcal
Fat	16.4 g
Carbohydrates	91.1g
Protein	21.6 g
Cholesterol	31 mg
Sodium	1182 mg

Ingredients

- 1 yam, peeled and diced
- 1 tbsp olive oil
- 3/4 lb. ground turkey
- 1/2 C. chopped sweet onion
- 1 clove garlic, minced
- 4 jalapeno peppers, seeded and minced
- 1 tbsp chili powder
- 1 tsp ground cumin
- 1/2 tsp Cajun seasoning
- 1/2 tsp salt
- 1/2 C. tomatillo salsa
- 1/2 C. chopped fresh cilantro
- 16 warm flour tortillas

Directions

1. In a microwave safe bowl, add the diced yam and microwave for about 5-7 minutes, stirring once in the middle way.
2. In a large skillet, heat the olive oil on medium heat and cook the turkey for about 5-7 minutes.
3. Add the onion, garlic, and jalapeño pepper and cook for about 7-10 minutes.
4. Stir in the chili powder, cumin, Cajun seasoning and salt and top with the salsa.
5. Fold in the yam and cook till the excess moisture is absorbed.
6. Top with the cilantro and serve with the warm tortillas.

RESTAURANT-STYLE
Salsa

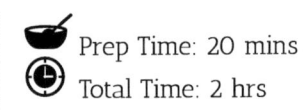

Prep Time: 20 mins
Total Time: 2 hrs

Servings per Recipe: 15
Calories   40 kcal
Fat   3 g
Carbohydrates   3.2g
Protein   0.6 g
Cholesterol   0 mg
Sodium   120 mg

Ingredients

10 fresh tomatillos, husks removed
3 cloves garlic
1 C. water
4 serrano chilis, stemmed
2 Poblano chilis, stemmed
3 tbsp vegetable oil
1 yellow onion, chopped

1 tsp coarse salt
1/4 C. chopped fresh cilantro
2 tbsp minced red onion
1 tbsp fresh lime juice

Directions

1. In a pan, add the tomatillos, garlic cloves and water on high heat and bring to a boil.
2. Reduce the heat to medium-low and simmer for about 15-20 minutes.
3. Set the broiler of your oven and arrange oven rack about 6-inches from the heating element.
4. Line a baking sheet with a piece of foil.
5. Cut the Serrano peppers and Poblano peppers in half from top to bottom.
6. Remove the stem, seeds and ribs.
7. Arrange the peppers, cut-side-down onto the prepared baking sheet.
8. Cook under the broiler for about 3-5 minutes.
9. Remove from the oven and transfer into a bowl.
10. Immediately with a plastic wrap, seal the bowl tightly and keep aside for about 5-7 minutes.
11. Remove the blackened skins from the peppers.
12. Add the peppers into the simmering tomatillos mixture and cook for about 5 minutes.
13. In a skillet, heat the vegetable oil on medium heat and sauté the yellow onion for about 7-10 minutes.

14. In a blender, add the yellow onions and tomatillo mixture and pulse till smooth.
15. Return the mixture into the skillet on medium-high heat and simmer for about 5-7 minutes.
16. Transfer the mixture into a bowl and keep aside to cool in room temperature.
17. After cooling, stir in the salt, cilantro, red onion and lime juice and serve.

WORKING WOMAN'S
Favorite Chili

Prep Time: 15 mins
Total Time: 3 hrs 20 mins

Servings per Recipe: 7
Calories   148 kcal
Fat   4.4 g
Carbohydrates   18.4g
Protein   10.7 g
Cholesterol   21 mg
Sodium   862 mg

Ingredients

1/2 lb. lean ground beef
1 (14 oz.) can tomato sauce
2 (6 oz.) cans tomato paste
3 stalks celery, chopped
1 C. canned diced tomatoes
1/2 onion, chopped
1/2 C. canned black beans, rinsed and drained
2 tbsp hot pepper sauce
1/2 tsp chili powder

Directions

1. Heat a large skillet on medium-high heat and cook the beef for about 5-7 minutes.
2. Drain the excess grease from the skillet.
3. Transfer the beef into a slow cooker crock.
4. Add the tomato sauce, tomato paste, celery, diced tomatoes, onion, black beans, hot pepper sauce and chili powder and mix well.
5. Set the slow cooker on High and cook for about 1 hour, stirring occasionally.
6. Now, set the slow cooker on Low and cook for about 2 hours, stirring occasionally.

Guadalajara Steak

Prep Time: 25 mins
Total Time: 55 mins

Servings per Recipe: 6
Calories   374 kcal
Fat   16.4 g
Carbohydrates   27.6 g
Protein   29.3 g
Cholesterol   58 mg
Sodium   944 mg

Ingredients

- 4 fresh tomatillos, husks removed
- 3 serrano chili peppers, seeded and chopped
- 1 clove garlic, peeled
- 3 C. water
- 6 slices turkey bacon
- 2 lb. flank steak, cut into 1/2-inch squares
- 4 tsp chicken bouillon granules
- 2 (15.5 oz.) cans pinto beans
- 1/2 onion, chopped
- 6 tbsp chopped fresh cilantro
- ground black pepper, to taste
- 1 lime, cut into 6 wedges

Directions

1. In a small pan, add the tomatillos, Serrano peppers, garlic and water on medium-high heat and bring to a boil.
2. Simmer, covered for about 10 minutes.
3. Remove from the heat and keep aside to cool.
4. Transfer the mixture into a blender and pulse till smooth.
5. Heat a large, deep skillet over medium-high heat and cook the bacon for about 10 minutes.
6. Transfer the bacon onto a paper towel lined plate to drain and then crumble it.
7. Heat a non-stick skillet on medium-high heat and cook the flank steak till browned completely.
8. Add the tomatillo mixture and bring to a boil, then stir in the chicken bouillon.
9. Reduce the heat to medium and simmer, covered for about 30-60 minutes.
10. Meanwhile in a pan, cook the pinto beans on medium heat till warm.
11. Add the bacon and pinto beans in the flank steak mixture and stir to combine.
12. Divide the mixture into serving bowls and serve with a garnishing of the onion, cilantro, black pepper and a lime wedge.

TRADITIONAL
Mexican Pie

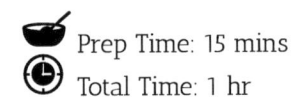

🥣 Prep Time: 15 mins
🕐 Total Time: 1 hr

Servings per Recipe: 6
Calories   289 kcal
Fat   19.2 g
Carbohydrates   18.2g
Protein   11.2 g
Cholesterol   142 mg
Sodium   545 mg

Ingredients

4 eggs
1/2 C. milk
1/4 C. chopped fresh cilantro
1 red bell pepper, diced
1 pinch salt
1 pinch ground black pepper
2 dashes jalapeno sauce
1 C. shredded Cheddar-Monterey Jack cheese blend
1 (4 oz.) can diced green chilis
1 tomatillo, diced
1 recipe pastry for a 9 inch single crust pie

Directions

1. Set your oven to 350 degrees F before doing anything else.
2. In a bowl, add the eggs and beat well.
3. Add the milk, cilantro, bell pepper, spices, cheese, chilis and tomatillo and stir to combine.
4. Place the tomatillo mixture into the pie shell.
5. Cook in the oven for about 45-50 minutes.
6. Remove from the oven and keep aside to cool in the room temperature.
7. Serve with a topping of the sour cream and salsa.

Authentic Latin Dinner Chicken

Prep Time: 10 mins
Total Time: 2 hrs 40 mins

Servings per Recipe: 4
Calories	366.8
Fat	29.1g
Cholesterol	78.9mg
Sodium	74.1mg
Carbohydrates	10.0g
Protein	17.7g

Ingredients

- 4 chicken thighs
- 1 lemon
- salt
- pepper
- 4 tbsp olive oil
- 1/4 white onion, diced
- 1 tbsp garlic clove, chopped
- 1 lb. tomatillo, dehusked and chopped
- 2 chipotle peppers
- 1 tbsp Mexican oregano

Directions

1. Season the chicken thighs with the salt and pepper and drizzle with the lemon juice.
2. Refrigerate for about 2 hours.
3. In a large skillet, heat the olive oil on medium heat and sauté the garlic and onion till tender.
4. Place the chicken, skin side down and cook for about 4-5 minutes per side.
5. Add the tomatillos, peppers, and oregano and simmer, covered for about 20 minutes.
6. Serve immediately.

SOUTHWESTERN Tomatillos

Prep Time: 20 mins
Total Time: 20 mins

Servings per Recipe: 1
Calories 59.9
Fat 4.6g
Cholesterol 13.3mg
Sodium 63.7mg
Carbohydrates 3.2g
Protein 2.0g

Ingredients

20 tomatillos
2/3 C. cheddar cheese, shredded
1/2 C. whole kernel corn
6 oz. cream cheese, softened
2 green onions, sliced (with tops)

1 tsp ground red chili pepper
ground red chili pepper (for garnish)

Directions

1. Cut a thin slice from stem ends of tomatillos.
2. With a small spoon, remove the pulp and seeds.
3. With a paper towel, blot the insides of each tomatillo.
4. In a bowl, add the cheddar cheese, corn, cream cheese, onions and 1 tsp of the ground red chilis and mix well.
5. Stuff the each tomatillo with the cheese mixture evenly and sprinkle with the ground red chilis.
6. Refrigerate, covered till serving.

Sizzling Skillet Shrimp

Prep Time: 10 mins
Total Time: 40 mins

Servings per Recipe: 4
Calories	300.5
Fat	16.1g
Cholesterol	160.9mg
Sodium	1027.2mg
Carbohydrates	16.8g
Protein	22.7g

Ingredients

- 2 tbsp vegetable oil
- 1 medium onion, chopped
- 1 - 2 jalapeno chili, seeded and minced
- 3 garlic cloves, thinly sliced
- 1 lb. tomatillo, chopped
- salt
- 1/2 C. clam juice
- 1 lb. shrimp, cleaned, deveined
- 1 C. cotija queso seco cheese
- 1/4 C. chopped cilantro
- lime juice
- black pepper

Directions

1. In an oven proof skillet heat the oil on medium-high heat and sauté the onions and jalapeños for about 5 minutes.
2. Add the garlic and sauté for about 1 minute and stir in the tomatillos.
3. Reduce the heat to medium and cook for about 10 minutes.
4. Meanwhile, set your oven to 425 degrees F.
5. Sprinkle salt over the tomatillos while cooking.
6. Add the clam juice and increase the heat and cook till the mixture reduce by half.
7. Stir in the cheese and shrimp and transfer into the oven.
8. Cook in the oven for about 10 minutes.
9. Remove the skillet from the oven and stir in the cilantro and lime juice.
10. Serve with a sprinkling of the freshly ground black pepper.

CANCUN
Breakfast

🥣 Prep Time: 30 mins
🕐 Total Time: 1 hr 5 mins

Servings per Recipe: 4
Calories   699.8
Fat   44.6g
Cholesterol   110.5mg
Sodium   1183.0mg
Carbohydrates   42.3g
Protein   34.0g

Ingredients

2 C. tomatillos, husked and chopped
1/2 C. Poblano chilis, roasted and chopped
1/4 C. yellow onion, minced
2 garlic cloves, minced
3/4 C. chicken broth
2 tbsp whipping cream
3 tbsp fresh cilantro, minced
salt and pepper
12 -16 stale corn tortillas, thick ones work the best

vegetable oil (for frying)
1 C. chorizo sausage, cooked and drained, optional
1/2 medium onion, sliced in thin rings
2 C. Monterey jack cheese
crema (garnish)

Directions

1. Set your oven to 350 degrees F before doing anything else.
2. For the sauce in a medium pan, mix together the tomatillos, chilis, chopped onion, garlic, broth and whipping cream and simmer for about 10 minutes.
3. In a blender, add the sauce mixture with cilantro, salt and pepper and pulse till smooth.
4. Cut each tortilla into sixths.
5. In a skillet, add about 1/2-inch of the oil on medium heat and fry the tortillas till chewy but not crispy.
6. In a shallow baking dish, arrange a layer of the tortillas, followed by half of the sauce, chorizo, onion, cheese and remaining sauce.
7. Cook in the oven for about 20-25 minutes.
8. Serve hot with a garnishing of the cream.

Salsa Festival

Prep Time: 10 mins
Total Time: 10 mins

Servings per Recipe: 1
Calories	58.5
Fat	0.9g
Cholesterol	0.0mg
Sodium	4.6mg
Carbohydrates	12.5g
Protein	1.5g

Ingredients

- 8 oz. tomatillos, husked, rinsed, and cut into 1/4-inch pieces
- 1/2 C. chopped red bell pepper
- 1/4 C. chopped red onion
- 1/4 C. chopped fresh cilantro
- 1 plum tomato, seeded and chopped
- 2 tbsp minced seeded jalapenos
- 2 tbsp fresh lime juice
- 2 tsp sugar
- 2 garlic cloves, minced
- salt
- pepper

Directions

1. Combine all Ingredients and mix well.

LATE JUNE
Salsa

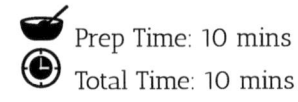

Prep Time: 10 mins
Total Time: 10 mins

Servings per Recipe: 1
Calories	88.7
Fat	2.4g
Cholesterol	0.0mg
Sodium	1168.9mg
Carbohydrates	17.4g
Protein	2.5g

Ingredients

1 lb. tomatillo, roughly chopped
3 serrano chilies, with seeds
3/4 C. fresh cilantro leaves
2 tbsp fresh lime juice
1 tsp sugar
1 tsp salt

Directions

1. In a blender, add all the Ingredients and pulse till smooth.

Mexican Cilantro Appetizer

Prep Time: 10 mins
Total Time: 25 mins

Servings per Recipe: 1
Calories   161.4
Fat   2.3g
Cholesterol   0.0mg
Sodium   847.9mg
Carbohydrates   30.8g
Protein   4.9g

Ingredients

- 1/4 lb. tomatillo
- 1/2 small green pepper, deseeded, cut into 1 inch pieces
- 1/4 C. fresh flat leaf parsley, chopped
- 1/4 C. fresh cilantro, chopped
- 1/2 jalapeno, destemmed, and deseeded
- 1 scallion, chopped
- 4 slices white bread, crust removed, and torn into pieces
- 1 C. water
- 1/2 tsp salt

Directions

1. Set the broiler of your oven.
2. Remove the stems and husks from the tomatillos and then rinse them.
3. Arrange the tomatillos onto a broiler pan and cook under the broiler till the skins begin to blacken.
4. Remove from the broiler and cut off any black spots.
5. In a blender, add the tomatillos and the remaining Ingredients and pulse till smooth.
6. In a pan, add the pureed mixture and cook till warmed.

CHIPOTLE Salmon

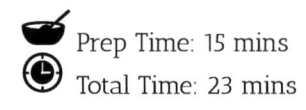

Prep Time: 15 mins
Total Time: 23 mins

Servings per Recipe: 4
Calories 331.3
Fat 15.6g
Cholesterol 77.4mg
Sodium 618.3mg
Carbohydrates 12.2g
Protein 36.4g

Ingredients

4 medium tomatillos, husked and rinsed
1/4 C. green onion, chopped
1/4 C. fresh cilantro, chopped
1 1/2 tbsp fresh lime juice
1 ripe avocado, seeded and diced
1 tsp jalapeno, seeded and minced
1 1/2 tbsp chili powder

1/2 tsp cumin
1 tbsp brown sugar
1 tsp kosher salt
4 (6 oz.) wild copper river salmon fillets

Directions

1. In a pan, add the tomatillo and enough water to cover and bring to a boil.
2. Simmer for about 5 minutes.
3. Remove the tomatillos and keep aside to cool. When cool, then chop them roughly.
4. In a large bowl, mix together the tomatillos, onion, cilantro, lime juice and salt.
5. Gently fold in the avocado and jalapeño.
6. Set your oven to 350 degrees.
7. In a bowl, mix together the chili powder, cumin, sugar and salt.
8. Coat the fish with the spice mix.
9. Heat a large oven-proof nonstick skillet on medium heat and cook the salmon rub side down for about 2 minutes.
10. Flip the fish and transfer the skillet into the oven and cook for about 5-6 minutes.
11. Transfer the fish fillets into the serving plates and serve with a topping of the salsa.

New Mexican Lunch Rice

Prep Time: 5 mins
Total Time: 6 mins

Servings per Recipe: 1
Calories	766.9
Fat	18.7g
Cholesterol	103.8mg
Sodium	1215.6mg
Carbohydrates	101.6g
Protein	50.2g

Ingredients

- 1 1/4 C. cooked brown rice
- 3/4 C. cooked chicken, cubed
- 1/4 C. Monterey jack cheese, grated
- 1/2 C. canned black beans, drained
- 1/4 C. frozen corn
- 1/4 C. tomatillo, finely chopped
- 1/3 C. bottled salsa

Directions

1. In a large microwave safe bowl, place the Ingredients in the order listed.
2. Cover the bowl and microwave for about 30-60 seconds.

CREAMY
Tomatillo Topping or Dip

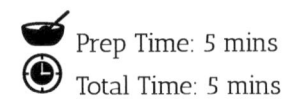

Prep Time: 5 mins
Total Time: 5 mins

Servings per Recipe: 8
Calories	101.2
Fat	9.2g
Cholesterol	57.0mg
Sodium	309.4mg
Carbohydrates	3.7g
Protein	1.8g

Ingredients

1 (4 oz.) cans green chilies
1 3/4 C. canned tomatillos, drained
1/4 C. cilantro leaf
3/4 C. heavy cream
1 egg
1 tsp salt

Directions

1. In a food processor, add all the Ingredients and pulse till smooth.
2. Cook your favorite enchiladas and burritos in this sauce.

Easy Chicken Stew

Prep Time: 15 mins
Total Time: 1 hr 20 mins

Servings per Recipe: 6
Calories   274.5
Fat   5.7g
Cholesterol   94.4mg
Sodium   317.9mg
Carbohydrates   30.1g
Protein   26.2g

Ingredients

- 1 medium onion, cut into 1/4 inch rounds
- 4 medium red potatoes, cut into 1/4 inch rounds
- 1/4 tsp salt
- 1 1/2 lb. boneless skinless chicken thighs
- 1 C. loosely packed fresh cilantro leaves
- 1 1/4 lb. tomatillos, with husks removed, washed, and cut into 1/4 inch rounds
- 1/4 C. sliced pickled jalapeno pepper

Directions

1. Set your oven to 400 degrees F before doing anything else.
2. In the bottom of 5-6 quart Dutch oven, arrange the onion slices, followed by the potatoes rounds and sprinkle with the salt.
3. Arrange the chicken over the potatoes, followed by cilantro, tomatillos, jalapeños and drizzle with the pickling liquid.
4. Cover the Dutch oven and cook in the oven for about 45 minutes.
5. Uncover and cook in the oven for about 15-20 minutes.
6. Serve hot with a garnishing of the more cilantro.

THE BEST
Salsa Ever!

Prep Time: 15 mins
Total Time: 15 mins

Servings per Recipe: 6
Calories   37.8
Fat   0.9g
Cholesterol   0.0mg
Sodium   12.1mg
Carbohydrates   7.5g
Protein   1.3g

Ingredients

2 medium tomatoes, quartered
6 medium tomatillos
1 small red onion, quartered
2 garlic cloves, pressed or minced
2 jalapeno peppers (seeded, roasted)
2 limes, juice of
1/4-1/2 C. fresh cilantro
2 tbsp ground cumin

1 pinch red pepper flakes
1/2 tsp ground coriander
1 tsp TABASCO® brand Chipotle Pepper Sauce
sea salt (to taste)
fresh ground pepper (to taste)

Directions

1. In a food processor, add all Ingredients and pulse till desired consistency.
2. This will be best for chips.

Tamale Cakes with Southwest Sauce

- Prep Time: 30 mins
- Total Time: 1 hr 7 mins

Servings per Recipe: 4
Calories 454.8
Fat 31.4g
Cholesterol 68.4mg
Sodium 635.0mg
Carbohydrates 43.2g
Protein 5.6g

Ingredients

SALSA VERDE
2 tomatillos, chopped (remove papery skin)
4 oz. mild green chilies
1 green onion, chopped
2 tbsp cilantro, fresh
1 1/4 tsp ground cumin
salt & fresh ground pepper
TOMATO SALSA
1 medium tomatoes, diced
1 tbsp Spanish onion, minced
1 tbsp cilantro, fresh minced
1/4 tsp lime juice
1/2 jalapeno, small minced
salt
fresh ground pepper
SOUTHWESTERN SAUCE
1/2 C. mayonnaise
1 tsp white vinegar
1 tsp water
3/4 tsp granulated sugar
1/2 tsp chili powder
1/4 tsp paprika
1/8 tsp cayenne pepper
1/8 tsp onion powder
salt
garlic powder
TAMALE CAKES
1 1/2 C. corn, sweet frozen
1/2 C. butter, softened
3 tbsp granulated sugar
1/8 tsp salt
1/2 C. masa harina (corn flour)
2 tbsp all-purpose flour
GARNISH
1/4 C. sour cream
1/2 avocado, chopped
2 tbsp cilantro, fresh chopped

Directions

1. For the Salsa Verde in a food processor, add all the Ingredients and pulse on high speed till well combined.
2. Transfer the mixture into a bowl and refrigerate, covered to chill.
3. For the tomato salsa in a bowl, mix together all the Ingredients and refrigerate, covered to chill.

4. For the Southwestern sauce in a small bowl, mix together all the Ingredients and refrigerate, covered to chill.
5. Set your oven to 400 degrees F.
6. For the Tamale cakes in a food processor, add about 1 C. of the frozen corn and pulse till pureed roughly.
7. In a bowl, add the pureed corn, softened butter, sugar and salt and with an electric mixer, blend till smooth.
8. Add the masa and flour and blend till well combined.
9. Fold in the remaining 1/2 C. of the frozen corn.
10. Make 3-inch patties from the mixture.
11. Place the patties onto a baking sheet in a single layer.
12. Cook in the oven for about 25-30 minutes.
13. Carefully flip the cakes and cook in the oven for about 5-7 minutes.
14. Spread about 1/4 the Salsa Verde onto a platter and top with the Tamale Cakes.
15. Serve with the topping of the sour cream.

South American Tacos

Prep Time: 10 mins
Total Time: 40 mins

Servings per Recipe: 5
Calories	756.8
Fat	28.7g
Cholesterol	58.9mg
Sodium	113.5mg
Carbohydrates	99.3g
Protein	31.2g

Ingredients

5 large potatoes, cubed
1 lb. lean ground beef
1/2 onion, chopped
salt and pepper, to taste
4 tomatillos, husked and quartered
1 garlic clove, peeled
1 jalapeno pepper, diced
1/2 C. fresh cilantro, chopped
3 avocados, halved with pits removed
10 (6 inch) corn tortillas

Directions

1. In a large pan of water, cook the potatoes and bring to a boil.
2. Cook, covered for about 10 minutes and then drain well.
3. Meanwhile, heat a large skillet on medium-high heat and cook the beef till browned completely.
4. Stir in the onion and cook till the onion becomes tender.
5. Drain the excess grease from the skillet and gently stir in the potatoes, salt and pepper.
6. In a blender, add the tomatillos, garlic, jalapeño, cilantro and avocado flesh and pulse till smooth.
7. Heat a skillet and cook the tortillas till warm and flexible.
8. Place the meat mixture over the tortilla and top with the tomatillo sauce.
9. Roll up each tortilla and serve.

SAN MIGUEL de Allende Shrimp

Prep Time: 20 mins
Total Time: 40 mins

Servings per Recipe: 4
Calories	354.4
Fat	24.8g
Cholesterol	282.9mg
Sodium	1066.2mg
Carbohydrates	8.6g
Protein	24.7g

Ingredients

FOR SAUCE
1/2 lb. tomatillo, husked
2 Poblano chilis, roasted and peeled
1/2 C. whipping cream
1 shallot, minced
1/4 C. butter, cut into pieces
salt

FOR THE GRILL
mesquite charcoal
hickory wood chunks, soaked and drained
SHRIMP
24 unshelled jumbo shrimp

Directions

1. In a blender, add the tomatillos and chilies and pulse till smooth.
2. In a skillet, add the pureed tomatillo mixture, cream and shallot on medium high heat and cook for about 4-5 minutes, stirring continuously.
3. Strain the sauce and return the pan on low heat.
4. Slowly, add the butter, 1 tbsp at a time and beat till well combined.
5. Stir in the salt and keep warm.
6. In a grill, heat the mesquite charcoal and hickory chunks till the coals become white.
7. Add more hickory chunks.
8. As soon as the smoke rises, push coals and chunks to one side of the grill.
9. Grease the grill generously.
10. Arrange shrimp onto 1 side of the grill (not over heat source) and smoke, covered for about 6-8 minutes.
11. Serve the grilled shrimp with the tomatillos sauce.

Southwestern Burgers

Prep Time: 30 mins
Total Time: 40 mins

Servings per Recipe: 6
Calories	1053.6
Fat	67.5g
Cholesterol	212.7mg
Sodium	3234.7mg
Carbohydrates	34.7g
Protein	79.1g

Ingredients

BURGERS
8 onion bread, sliced & toasted
1 tbsp coriander
1 tbsp garlic powder
1 tbsp cumin
8 slices Monterey jack pepper cheese
8 boneless skinless chicken breasts
1 C. tomatillo salsa
1 C. guacamole
1 C. garlic aioli
1/2 C. chopped green chili
1 lb. turkey bacon
leafy green lettuce
2 tomatoes, sliced
1 small onion, finely sliced
TOMATILLO SALSA
1 small sweet onion, chopped
2 garlic cloves, peeled
2 dried chipotle chilis
1/2 bunch fresh cilantro, leaves and stems
1/2 C. water
2 tsp coarse salt

1/2-1 tsp sugar
1/2 lb. tomatillo, husked, washed, and roasted
1 lime, juice of
GUACAMOLE
3 medium avocados, seeded peeled, and diced
3 garlic cloves, minced
1 onion, finely minced
1 C. green chili, chopped
2 tbsp cilantro, chopped
1 lime, juice of
3 medium ripe tomatoes, chopped
salt and pepper
chili pepper
GARLIC AIOLI
1/2 C. mayonnaise
1 tsp finely chopped garlic
1 tbsp lemon juice
1/2 tsp hot sauce
2 tbsp chopped fresh coriander
salt, to taste
fresh ground pepper, to taste

Directions

1. One day before cooking, prepare the chipotle tomatillo salsa.
2. In a bowl, mix together all the salsa Ingredients and refrigerate till serving.
3. 2 hours before serving, prepare the guacamole and garlic Aioli.

4. For guacamole in a bowl, mix together all the Ingredients and refrigerate till serving.
5. For garlic Aioli in a bowl, mix together all the Ingredients and refrigerate till serving.
6. For chicken in a flat plate, mix together the coriander, garlic powder and cumin.
7. Coat the chicken breasts with the spice mixtures evenly and transfer onto a clean plate.
8. With a plastic wrap, cover the chicken breasts and refrigerate for about 1 hour.
9. Heat a frying pan and fry bacon till crisp and transfer onto a clean plate.
10. With a plastic wrap, cover the bacon and refrigerate before cooking.
11. Tear up lettuce and cut the tomatoes and onion in slices.
12. Arrange the lettuce, tomato and onion slices onto a serving platter and with a plastic wrap, cover and refrigerate.
13. Set your grill for medium-high heat and lightly, grease the grill grate.
14. Cook the chicken breasts on the grill for about 5 minutes from both sides.
15. Meanwhile, coat the bread slices with the olive oil lightly.
16. Cook the bread slices on the grill till toasted.
17. In the last minute, place 1 Pepper Jack cheese slices over each breast.
18. Arrange the chicken breasts over each toasted bread slice, followed by bacon, onion, chopped green chili, salsa, guacamole, garlic Aioli, tomato and lettuce.
19. Serve immediately.

Vegetarian Mexican Casserole

Prep Time: 1 hr
Total Time: 1 hr 25 mins

Servings per Recipe: 6
Calories	224.1
Fat	10.8g
Cholesterol	24.1mg
Sodium	288.3mg
Carbohydrates	23.7g
Protein	10.2g

Ingredients

TOMATILLO SAUCE
1/2 C. water
1/2 large red onion, thinly sliced
1/2 tsp salt
1/4 tsp cayenne pepper
1/2 large green bell pepper, seeded, deveined and coarsely chopped
1 lb. tomatillos, husked
1 serrano chili, seeded and chopped
1 pinch sugar
FILLING
1 tbsp olive oil
1/2 red onion, diced
1/8 tsp salt
1/8 tsp cayenne pepper

3 large garlic cloves, minced
1/2 bell pepper (yellow, seeded and chopped)
1/2 zucchini, diced
1/2 tsp ground cumin
3 - 4 mushrooms, sliced
1 C. fresh corn kernel
1 C. cooked black beans
1 tbsp chopped fresh cilantro
9 - 10 corn tortillas
1/2 C. light sour cream
2 C. shredded Monterey jack cheese
2 tbsp chopped fresh cilantro

Directions

1. For tomatillo sauce in a large pan, mix together the water, onion, salt and cayenne and bring to a boil.
2. Reduce the heat and simmer, covered for about 5 minutes.
3. Add the bell pepper, tomatillos and chilies and simmer, covered for about 10-15 minutes.
4. With an immersion blender, blend the mixture till pureed.
5. For filling in a large skillet, heat the oil on medium-high heat and sauté the red onion, salt and cayenne for about 8 minutes.
6. Add the garlic, bell pepper, zucchini and cumin and cook for about 5 minutes.
7. Add the mushrooms, corn and beans and cook for about 5 minutes.

8. Stir in the cilantro and remove from heat.
9. Set your oven to 400 degrees f.
10. In the bottom of a 9x9 baking dish, place about 1 C. of the tomatillo sauce.
11. Heat a frying pan on medium-high heat and heat the tortillas till pliable.
12. Arrange the tortillas onto a smooth surface.
13. Place about 1 tbsp of the sour cream in the center of each tortilla, followed by 3 tbsp of the filling and finally 2 tbsp of the grated cheese.
14. Roll the tortillas up and arrange, seam side down over the tomatillo sauce in the baking dish.
15. Top with the remaining sauce evenly and sprinkle with the cheese.
16. With a piece of the foil, cover the baking dish and cook in the oven for about 20 minutes.
17. Remove the foil and cook in the oven for about 5-7 minutes.
18. Serve with a sprinkling of the cilantro.

Mexico City Green Enchiladas

Prep Time: 15 mins
Total Time: 45 mins

Servings per Recipe: 4
Calories   413.2
Fat   20.9g
Cholesterol   23.2mg
Sodium   1644.7mg
Carbohydrates   43.2g
Protein   15.8g

Ingredients

- 2 bone-in chicken breast halves
- 2 C. chicken broth
- 1/4 white onion
- 1 garlic clove
- 2 tsp salt
- 1 lb. fresh tomatillo, husks removed
- 5 Serrano peppers
- 1/4 white onion
- 1 garlic clove
- 1 pinch salt
- 12 corn tortillas
- 1/4 C. vegetable oil
- 1 C. crumbled queso fresco
- 1/2 white onion, chopped
- 1 bunch fresh cilantro, chopped

Directions

1. In a pan, mix together the chicken breast, chicken broth, one quarter onion, and a clove of garlic and 2 tsp of the salt and bring to a boil.
2. Boil for about 20 minutes.
3. Transfer the chicken into plate and keep aside to cool, then shred it.
4. Remove the onion and garlic and reserve the broth.
5. In a pan, add the tomatillos and Serrano chilis and enough water to cover and bring to boil.
6. Boil till the tomatillos changes into a dull, army green color.
7. Strain the tomatillos and chilis completely.
8. In a blender, add the tomatillo mixture, another quarter piece of onion, 1 garlic clove, a pinch of salt and enough reserved chicken broth to just cover the veggies in the blender by 1-inch and pulse till smooth.
9. In a medium pan, add the salsa and bring to a low boil.
10. In a frying pan, heat the oil and slightly fry the tortillas, one at a time.
11. Transfer the tortillas onto a paper towel lined plate to drain.

12. Finally, dip the fried tortillas in boiled salsa till they become soft again.
13. In each plate, place 3 tortillas.
14. Top the tortillas with shredded chicken, followed by extra green sauce, crumbled cheese, chopped onion and chopped cilantro.

Rural Mexican Breakfast Eggs

Prep Time: 1 hr
Total Time: 1 hr

Servings per Recipe: 4
Calories 549.2
Fat 32.0g
Cholesterol 476.9mg
Sodium 528.9mg
Carbohydrates 34.6g
Protein 32.6g

Ingredients

SAUCE
1 dried chipotle chili
1 jalapeno pepper, stemmed and seeded
1 lb. tomatillo, husked
2 medium tomatoes, stemmed
1 tsp vegetable oil
1 tsp dried oregano
1 tsp dried marjoram
1 tbsp lime juice
salt and pepper, to taste

2 tbsp cilantro (optional)
ASSEMBLY
8 corn tortillas (6 inches)
1/2 lb. Monterey jack cheese, shredded
8 eggs
1/2 C. onion, white, finely diced
3 tbsp Parmesan cheese, grated
4 tbsp cilantro, chopped (optional)

Directions

1. Set your oven to 450 degrees F before doing anything else.
2. In a pan, add the chipotle pepper and jalapeño pepper and enough water to cover and bring to a boil.
3. Remove from the heat and keep aside for about 30 minutes. Drain well.
4. Meanwhile in a shallow metal baking dish, place the tomatillos and tomatoes.
5. Cook in the oven for about 15-20 minutes.
6. Remove the baking dish without turning off the oven.
7. In a blender, add the tomatillo mixture, drained peppers, oil, oregano, marjoram, lime juice, salt, pepper and cilantro and pulse till smooth.
8. Place the tortillas on a large baking sheet and top with the cheese evenly.
9. Cook in the oven for about 3 minutes.
10. Meanwhile, fry the eggs till desired doneness.
11. Place an egg over each tortilla and top with a generous tbsp of sauce, onions, parmesan cheese and cilantro.

SAKURA'S
Japanese Salsa

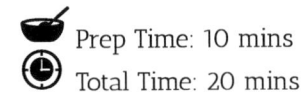

Prep Time: 10 mins
Total Time: 20 mins

Servings per Recipe: 8
Calories   34.7
Fat   0.7g
Cholesterol   0.0mg
Sodium   4.9mg
Carbohydrates   6.9g
Protein   1.2g

Ingredients

20 dried chilies, Japones (Japanese Chili Peppers)
6 garlic cloves, chopped
1 C. cilantro, chopped
1 small onion

15 tomatillos
5 green onions, chopped

Directions

1. Heat a hot cast iron frying pan, and cook the chili Japones till toasted.
2. Peel the papery skin off the tomatillos and boil in the water for about 10-15 minutes.
3. In a food processor, add the toasted chilies, garlic, onion and cooked tomatillos and pulse till well combined and chilies are tiny flecks.
4. Transfer the mixture into a container and stir in the chopped green onions and chopped cilantro.
5. Refrigerate to store.

Tamale Bake

Prep Time: 20 mins
Total Time: 1 hr 25 mins

Servings per Recipe: 4
Calories 802.7
Fat 45.4g
Cholesterol 108.0mg
Sodium 1264.2mg
Carbohydrates 50.9g
Protein 49.2g

Ingredients

FOR THE TAMALE DOUGH
2 C. masa harina flour
2 C. chicken broth
2/3 C. vegetable shortening
1/2 tsp salt
1/2 tsp sugar
1 tsp baking powder
FOR THE FILLING
1 1/4 lb. ground turkey breast
1 green bell pepper, chopped
1/2 yellow onion, chopped
1 green chili pepper, minced
2 tomatillos, chopped
1/2 C. cilantro, chopped
3 oz. Monterey jack cheese, grated
1 (1 1/4 oz.) packages taco seasoning mix
2 tsp chili powder
1 tsp cumin
1 tsp oregano
1/2 tsp paprika
1/2 tsp salt
cracked pepper
Monterey jack cheese, grated, for garnish
cilantro, torn, for garnish

Directions

1. Heat a large skillet on medium-high heat and cook the turkey for about 4-5 minutes.
2. Drain the excess grease from the skillet.
3. Add the green bell pepper, onion, green chili, tomatillos and cilantro and cook till softened.
4. Stir in the taco seasoning mix, chili powder, cumin, oregano, paprika, salt and pepper.
5. Reduce the heat to low and simmer for about 10 minutes.
6. Set your oven to 350 degrees F.
7. Meanwhile, in a bowl, add the vegetable shortening and with an electric mixer, beat on low speed till fluffy.
8. In another bowl, mix together the masa harina flour, salt, sugar and baking powder.
9. Add the chicken broth and with your hands, mix till well combined.
10. Add the flour mixture into the vegetable shortening and mix till a dough is formed.

11. In the bottom of a round casserole dish, place half of the masa harina dough evenly.
12. Place the turkey filling mixture over the dough and sprinkle with Monterey jack cheese.
13. Top with the remaining masa harina dough evenly.
14. Arrange the casserole dish
15. With a piece of the foil, cover the casserole dish and cook in the oven for about 55 minutes.
16. Now, set the oven to 425 degrees F.
17. Remove the foil and cook in the oven for about 10 minutes.
18. Remove from the oven and serve with a topping of the Monterey jack cheese and torn cilantro.

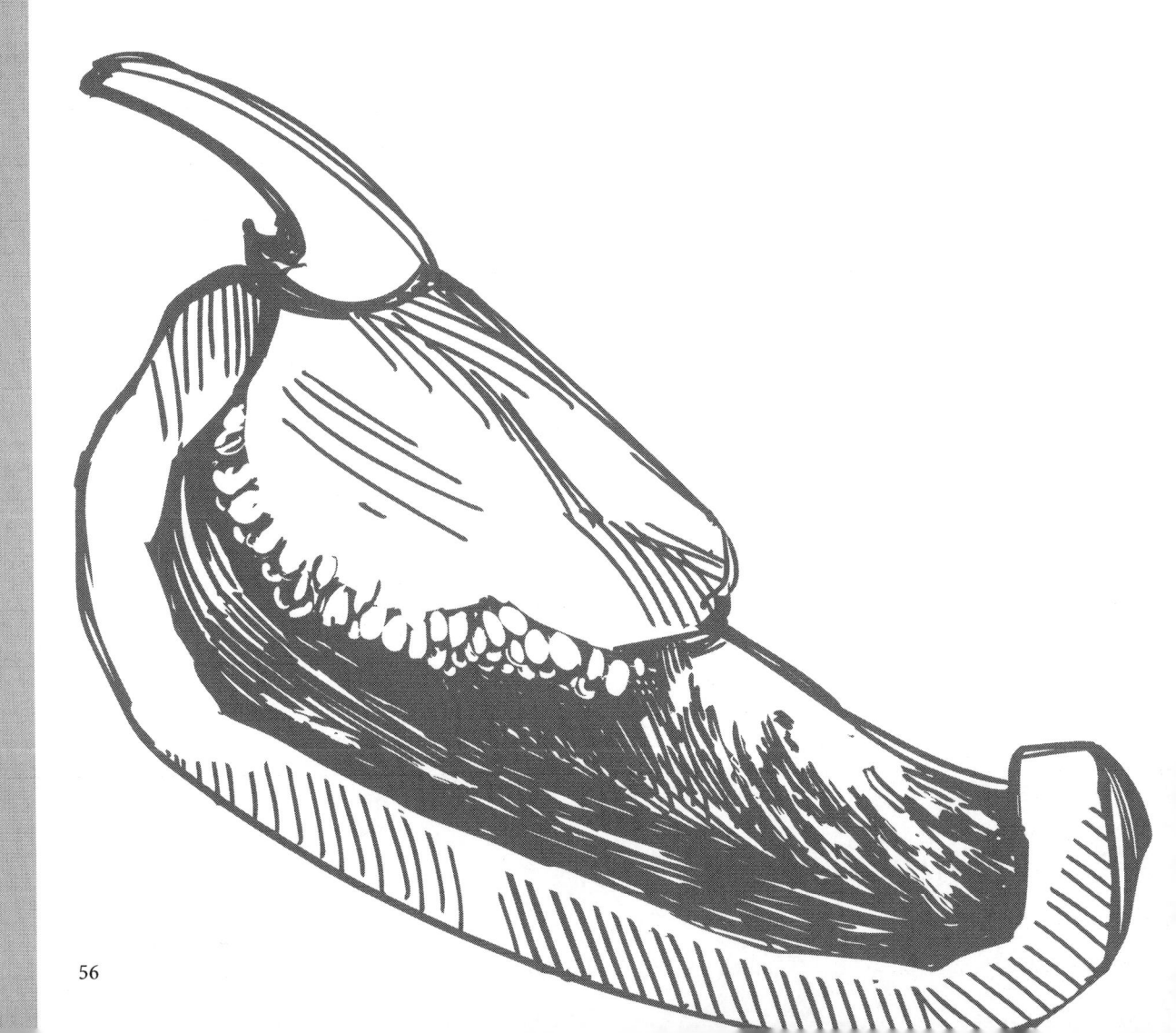

Orange Serrano Salmon on Grill

Prep Time: 15 mins
Total Time: 30 mins

Servings per Recipe: 6
Calories 293.3
Fat 11.4g
Cholesterol 98.5mg
Sodium 129.3mg
Carbohydrates 10.1g
Protein 38.7g

Ingredients

SALSA
1 navel orange, peeled, segmented
2 lemons, peeled, segmented
2 tsp seeded serrano chilies, minced
3/4 C. canned tomatillo, diced
1/2 C. red onion, diced
1/4 C. cilantro, chopped
1/2 tsp sugar
1 tsp fresh oregano

salt and pepper
SALMON
2 1/2 lb. fresh salmon fillets, skinless
2 tbsp vegetable oil
2 tbsp lemon juice
salt and pepper

Directions

1. Set your grill for medium-high heat and lightly, grease the grill grate.
2. Chop the orange and lemon segments roughly, retaining all the accumulate juice.
3. In a bowl, add the citrus fruit, juice and remaining salsa Ingredients and toss to coat well.
4. Refrigerate till before serving.
5. For salmon in a large bowl, add the oil, lemon juice, salt and pepper and mix till well combined.
6. Coat the salmon with the oil mixture generously.
7. Cook the salmon fillets on the grill for about 8 minutes, flipping once.
8. Serve the salmon with a topping of the salsa.

MEXICAN
Mango Salsa

Prep Time: 10 mins
Total Time: 10 mins

Servings per Recipe: 6
Calories	67.4
Fat	0.2g
Cholesterol	0.0mg
Sodium	155.1mg
Carbohydrates	14.6g
Protein	2.7g

Ingredients

1 C. canned black beans, rinsed and drained
1 medium ripe mango, peeled and chopped
1 medium tomatillo, paper covering discarded and diced
1/2 medium red onion, chopped
1/4 C. lime juice
1/4 C. fresh cilantro, chopped
1/4 tsp black pepper

Directions

1. In a bowl, add all the Ingredients and mix.
2. Refrigerate to chill before serving.

Deep Fried Avocado

Prep Time: 15 mins
Total Time: 25 mins

Servings per Recipe: 12
Calories	123 kcal
Fat	4.5 g
Carbohydrates	17.2g
Protein	3.8 g
Cholesterol	18 mg
Sodium	97 mg

Ingredients

- 1 avocado, sliced into 12 strips
- 1 C. all-purpose flour
- 1 egg, beaten
- 1 C. dry bread crumbs
- 2 tbsps grated Parmesan cheese, or as needed
- 3 tbsps sour cream
- 2 tbsps garlic powder
- 1 tbsp tomatillo salsa
- 1 dash chili-garlic sauce

Directions

1. Set your oven to 450 degrees before doing anything else.
2. Get a bowl and add in your flour.
3. Get a 2nd bowl for your eggs.
4. Get a 3rd bowl for your bread crumbs.
5. Coat your pieces of avocado first with flour, then in the eggs, and finally in the crumbs.
6. Layer all the avocadoes on a cookie sheet coated with nonstick spray then top everything with the parmesan.
7. Cook the contents in the oven for 12 mins.
8. Get a 4th bowl, combine: sriracha, sour cream, tomatillo salsa, and garlic powder.
9. Dip your pieces of avocado in the sriracha mix.
10. Enjoy.

CHICKEN TORTILLAS with Spicy Chocolate Sauce

Prep Time:	30 mins
Total Time:	1 hr 55 mins

Servings per Recipe: 4
Calories   739 kcal
Fat   34.8 g
Carbohydrates   77.7g
Protein   35.4 g
Cholesterol   101 mg
Sodium   2707 mg

Ingredients

- 2 tbsps lard
- 1/2 onion, sliced
- 2 cloves garlic, sliced
- 1 tsp salt
- 1 tbsp cumin seeds
- 2 Poblano peppers, seeded and thinly sliced
- 2 Anaheim peppers, seeded and thinly sliced
- 4 skinless, boneless chicken thighs, cut into chunks
- 4 C. chicken broth
- 2 C. chicken broth
- 4 dried guajillo chilis, stemmed and seeded
- 2 dried ancho chilis, stemmed and seeded
- 1 corn tortilla, cut into 1-inch strips
- 4 tomatoes, cut in half crosswise
- 3 tomatillos, cut in half crosswise
- 2 tbsps lard
- 1/2 onion, sliced
- 5 cloves garlic, sliced
- 2 tsps cumin seeds
- 2 C. chicken broth
- salt to taste
- 1 tsp white sugar, or more to taste
- 3 oz. dark chocolate, coarsely chopped
- 12 corn tortillas
- 1/2 bunch fresh cilantro, coarsely chopped
- 1/2 C. crumbled queso fresco

Directions

1. In a large pan, melt lard on medium heat and sauté 1/2 of the onion, 2 garlic cloves, Anaheim peppers, Poblano peppers, 1 tbsp of cumin seeds and salt for about 5-8 minutes.
2. Stir in the chicken thighs and 4 C. of broth.
3. Cook the mix covered for about 40 minutes.
4. In another pan, heat 2 C. of broth for about 5 minutes or till it just begins to simmer.
5. Heat a nonstick skillet on medium-high heat and toast the ancho chilis and guajillo chilis for about 3-4 minutes.
6. In a blender, add toasted chilis, tortilla strips and hot broth.

7. Keep the mix aside for about 10 minutes and then pulse till smooth.
8. In the same dry skillet, add tomatillos and tomatoes on medium-high heat and cook for about 3-4 minutes from both sides or till blackened and soft.
9. In a large skillet, melt the remaining 2 tbsps of lard on medium heat and sauté the remaining 1/2 of onion, 5 garlic cloves and 2 tbsps of cumin seeds for about 5-8 minutes.
10. Transfer the onion mixture into a blender with the chili mixture and pulse till smooth then transfer everything into another large pan on medium heat.
11. Stir in the remaining 2 C. of broth, chocolate, sugar and salt and bring to a gentle boil.
12. Cook, stirring continuously for about 5 minutes.
13. Toast the tortillas in a dry skillet for about 2-3 minutes from both sides or till soft.
14. Place 1/3 C. of chicken mixture in each tortilla and then roll them.
15. Place 3 tortillas on serving plates and top them with about 1/3 C. of chocolate sauce, cilantro and queso fresco.

MEXICAN STYLE
Salad Dressing

Prep Time: 15 mins
Total Time: 15 mins

Servings per Recipe: 12
Calories   49 kcal
Fat   0.1 g
Carbohydrates   < 8.4g
Protein   2.8 g
Cholesterol   7 mg
Sodium   405 mg

Ingredients

3 tomatillos, husked and quartered
1/2 bunch cilantro
2 pickled jalapeno peppers
1 (16 oz.) container fat-free sour cream
2 (1 oz.) packages ranch dressing mix

Directions

1. Blend the following in a blender for 1 min: jalapenos, cilantro, and tomatillos.
2. Now get a bowl, combine: ranch dressing, and sour cream.
3. Add in your green sauce, a quarter of your jalapeno mix, and stir everything together.
4. Taste the dressing and add more ranch mix (if necessary) then stir.
5. Continue to add in the jalapeno mix until the dressing suits your tastes.
6. Enjoy.

ENJOY THE RECIPES?

KEEP ON COOKING WITH 6 MORE FREE COOKBOOKS!

Visit our website and simply enter your email address to join the club and receive your 6 cookbooks.

http://booksumo.com/magnet

https://www.instagram.com/booksumopress/

https://www.facebook.com/booksumo/

Made in the
USA
Middletown, DE